A User's Guide to OLD AGE

Wisdom for Facing the Trials of Growing Older

Jo Elder and M.I. Wiser

Illustrations by Janora Bayot

One More Press
Lake Oswego, Oregon

Printed in the United States of America

Copyright © 1992 by Jo Elder & M.I. Wiser
Revised edition © 1993 by Jo Elder & M.I. Wiser

Library of Congress Cataloging-in-Publication Data

Elder, Jo -
    A user's guide to old age: "wisdom for facing the trials of
growing older" / by Jo Elder and M.I. Wiser; illustrations by Janora Bayot
        p.   cm.
    Includes index.
    ISBN 0-941361-98-5 : $6.50
    1. Old age — United States. I. Wiser, M.I., -
II. Title.
HQ1064.U5E396   1992
305.26'0973 — dc20   92-27867
                                                           CIP

One More Press
P.O. Box 1885
Lake Oswego, OR 97035
(503) 697-7964

A User's Guide to Old Age

Introduction

Old Age is an experience we can all hope to share.

Perhaps "hope" is not the most accurate word to use here—
"dread" or "resignation" come closer to the feelings many
people express at the prospect. But, considering the alternative,
most of us somehow allow ourselves to be swept along into Old
Age without a great deal of protest. We look the other way,
watch our friends turn grey and try to feel confident that we are
bucking the tide.

Suddenly, though, we find ourselves **there**. We wake up one morning and discover, to our surprise, bewilderment, and perhaps dismay, that we are what you might call "old". We have arrived at the portals of Old Age all by ourselves, without as much as a road map to give us direction. It's a prospect that's intriguing to the adventurous, yet a little overwhelming to most.

But wouldn't Old Age be a whole lot easier with a set of guidelines to ease us around the pitfalls and past the problems that mark our path? If only Old Age came equipped with a handbook, to smooth our transition into the land of the senior discounts, retirement pensions and creaky joints! What we need is an instruction manual, to make sure we're getting full use, complete enjoyment and, of course, our money's worth out of this brand new venture, Old Age.

Well, now it's here— **A User's Guide to Old Age**, designed for those of us who think we may be getting close, those who've already crossed the line into the category of Senior Citizen, and those who are just simply planning ahead. Pessimists, beware: this is no gloomy tome. It's a lighthearted book filled with humor and hope, wisdom, wealth and wellness. It can't show you how to turn back the clock, but it certainly will prove that Old Age is not to be feared but to be lived with laughter and exuberance.

We wish you a long, happy and rewarding Old Age!

Jo Elder
M.I.Wiser

*To those who have gone before us and
to those who will follow us into
Old Age.*

1 ✳ Aging is one experience we all share.

2 ✳ *"Whenever a man's friends begin to compliment him about looking young, he may be sure that they think he is growing old."*

Washington Irving

3 ✳ Laugh at life; you're a survivor.

4 ❋ Call an old friend.

5 ❋ Share a laugh with someone.

6 ❋ *"To be seventy years **young** is sometimes far more cheerful and hopeful than to be forty years **old**."*

Oliver Wendell Holmes

7 ✳ Each day do at least one nice thing for someone else — and one nice thing for yourself.

8 ✳ Make a list of things that would make your day perfect. Try to include at least one item from your list each and every day.

9 ✳ Listen to new ideas.

10 ❋ Be open-minded. Fossils don't have very much fun.

11 ❋ *"Curiosity is one of the most permanent and certain characteristics of a vigorous intellect."*

Dr. Samuel Johnson

12 ❋ Go back to school.

13 ❋ No matter how old you are, you're younger than you'll ever be.

14 ❋ *"We can no longer wait around for the ideal opportunity. If we have not achieved our early dream, we must either find new ones or see what we can salvage from the old."*
Rosalynn Carter

15 ✳ Begin each day by setting a goal.

16 ✳ Effective goals don't begin with the words, "Someday I'll...." Those are words for daydreams.

17 ✳ Reward yourself each time you reach a goal.

18 ✳ Be on the lookout for opportunity. It doesn't always knock.

19 ✳ Explore life.

20 ✳ *"Growing old is more like a bad habit which a busy man has no time to form."*

André Malraux

21 ❊ Old age: a time when you're sure you can do as much as you always did, but you'd rather not.

22 ❊ Plan an adventure.

23 ❊ Travel to new places, experience new thoughts, develop new ideas.

24 ✳ *"I advise thee to visit thy relatives and friends but I advise thee not to live too near to them."*

> Thomas Fuller
> 18th century physician.

25 ✳ Spend the day with your grandchildren.

26 ❋ Teach your grandchildren how to read a road map.

27 ❋ Stop to read historical roadside markers.

28 ❋ Establish your own special Grandchildren's Day, then celebrate!

29 ❋ Attend a high school play or band concert.

30 ❋ Hire a preteen to teach you the latest jargon. You do want to be "totally with it", don't you?

31 ✳ If you like roller coasters and ferris wheels, invite along a child whose parents just don't have the stomach for rides.

32 ❋ Smile a lot— a smile is often the best part of a day.

33 ❋ Optimists live longer than pessimists. Did you know that optimism is an acquired habit?

34 ❋ Stick around happy, positive people.

35 ✳ Spend as little time as possible with gloomy people.

36 ✳ Enthusiasm is contagious — spread it around.

37 ✳ Being optimistic doesn't mean you have to be complacent.

38 ❋ Listen to what you say. Guard
against negativity in your words.

39 ❋ Say five positive things every day.

40 ❋ Put a quarter or dollar in a jar every
time you hear yourself mention
your aches, pains or other physical
shortcomings.

41 ✳ Think positive thoughts: if your ankles ache when you wake up, at least it saves you from having to bend over to see if they're still there.

42 ✳ So your joints creak? Just hum a little louder.

43 ✳ Studies have shown that a moderate
weight-lifting program can help
preserve bone and muscle strength
as you age.

44 ✳ Move with as much energy and vigor
as you can. You'll look and feel
younger.

45 ✳ Start a walking group.

46 ✳ Buy the most comfortable walking shoes you can find.

47 ✳ Plan walks to look at historic buildings. The local historical society or library is a great place to learn their history.

48 ❋ Treat yourself to a massage.

49 ❋ Old age is when you stop feeling your oats and begin feeling your corns.

50 ❋ Treat yourself to a nap.

51 ❋ *"Although old age is creeping on*
To all its troubles I'm resigned.
My joints may stiffen but I'll not.
Have rheumatism in my mind."
Rebecca McCann

52 ❋ If there's a Senior Center nearby, join
in a few activities.

53 ✳ Be a newspaper clipper — send articles of interest to family and friends.

54 ✳ Write articles for the local newspaper.

55 ✳ Help write down your community's history.

56 ✳ Become a "regular" at your local library.

57 ✳ Keep a list of books you've read, as well as those you'd like to read.

58 ✳ Write book reviews for your local paper or library newsletter.

59 ✳ Read a magazine you've never tried before.

60 ✳ Keep a journal.

61 ✳ Trace your family tree.

62 ✳ Tape record your memories.

63 ❋ Expand your horizons.

64 ❋ Write a family song.

65 ❋ Design a family crest.

66 ❋ Start a family tradition — you get
to choose it!

67 ✳ Assemble a notebook of your all-time favorite recipes.

68 ✳ Try a new and different food.

69 ✳ If you've never eaten cactus, or tofu or squid, be adventurous — order something new when you see it on a menu.

70 ❋ Set aside one night a week for an Around-the-World Meal— one night try a Greek entrée, next week Mexican or Indian dishes.

71 ❋ Even if you live alone, cook meals. Freeze the extra portions for those nights when you have a full schedule.

72 ✳ If you live alone, alternate cooking dinner with a neighbor. You both get days off and someone to appreciate your efforts.

73 ✳ Bake a cake. If you can't eat it, surprise someone.

74 ✳ Have a picnic.

75 ❋ Want to get to know your neighbors?
Suggest a neighborhood potluck.

76 ❋ Treat your grandchildren, one at a
time, to a very special meal out.

77 ❋ Have an afternoon tea party once a
week. Invite a new or favorite
friend.

78 ✳ Celebrate every little anniversary.

79 ✳ *"If a man does not make new acquaintances as he advances through life, he will soon find himself alone."*
Dr. Samuel Johnson

80 ✳ Old age is when your descendants outnumber your friends.

81 ❊ Make new friends but keep the old.

82 ❊ Political campaign offices are a great place to meet people who think the way you do. Volunteer your help.

83 ❊ *"I never found the companion that was so companionable as solitude."*
        Henry David Thoreau

84 ❊ *"The happiest of all lives is a busy solitude."*

Voltaire

85 ❊ Make a list of things you'd like to do but think you couldn't possibly accomplish. Figure out a way to do at least one of them.

86 ✳ If you start to feel unloved, unwanted and unneeded, stop right now. There are those in this world who need the skills and talents that you have to offer. Challenge yourself to find your niche.

87 ✳ You're never too old to make the world a better place.

88 ❋ Volunteer to do something for your community.

89 ❋ Give historic tours.

90 ❋ Offer to teach living history at your local school.

91 ❋ Share your craft skills.

92 ✳ Teach a class in whatever you know best.

93 ✳ Volunteer to work with children.

94 ✳ Stuff envelopes for the candidate of your choice.

95 ✳ Join the church choir.

96 ✳ Be someone's best friend.

97 ✳ Learn to hug.

98 ✳ Sing love songs in the shower.

99 ✳ Love is the best antidote for old age.

100 ✳ Be an incurable romantic.

101 ✳ Send someone flowers.

102 ✳ Wear sexy lingerie.

103 ✳ Learn to give a great massage.

104 ❋ Be a little unpredictable — give someone a pleasant surprise.

105 ❋ Look for a four-leaf clover.

106 ❋ Say "I love you" often.

107 ❋ Never take a friendship for granted.

108 ✳ Did you take your spouse for granted today?

109 ✳ Share a secret.

110 ✳ Keep those secrets you're asked to keep.

111 ✳ Stay away from gossip.

112 ❋ Beware of snap judgments.

113 ❋ If there's anything worse than a
closed mind, it's an open mouth to
go along with it.

114 ❋ Grudges are just about the heaviest
weights you can carry around.
Dump them.

115 ✳ *"I did not attend his funeral but I wrote a nice letter saying I approved of it."*
Mark Twain

116 ✳ *"Always forgive your enemies; nothing annoys them so much."*
Oscar Wilde

117 ❋ Can you afford to have an enemy? Friends add to your stock of happiness and well-being; enemies deplete it.

118 ❋ Learn to forgive, then keep in practice.

119 ❋ Learn when it's best to forget.

120 ✳ *"'I can forgive but I cannot forget' is only another way of saying, 'I cannot forgive'."*

H.W. Beecher

121 ✳ Sometimes forgetting can be even harder than remembering.

122 ✳ Never go to bed angry.

123 ❊ A sense of humor is the best life preserver when the going gets rough.

124 ❊ If you've never learned to laugh at yourself, it's a good time to start.

125 ❊ Find the joy in life — or make your own.

126 ✳ Make every day special in at least one way.

127 ✳ Lie on the grass under a tree and enjoy the world around you.

128 ✳ How long has it been since you've seen the circus?

129 ❊ Never miss a parade.

130 ❋ Spend your money and enjoy it.
Don't worry about saving it for
your offspring to inherit.

131 ❋ Never put off a vacation.

132 ❋ Let a trustworthy neighbor know
when you'll be away on a trip.

133 ❋ Trust others, but bring your own deck of cards.

134 ❋ Be cautious about choosing advisors.

135 ❋ *"We are inclined to believe those whom we do not know because they have never deceived us."*
Dr. Samuel Johnson

136 ✳ Learn all about the latest scams and con games aimed at seniors — and find out how to avoid becoming a victim.

137 ✳ Check references carefully before hiring a contractor.

138 ✳ Be sceptical.

139 ✳ Avoid hiring contractors or
maintenance workers by the hour;
get a written price for the whole job.

140 ✳ Get at least two estimates for major
repairs.

141 ✳ Don't sign any contract on the spot.

142 ✳ If you feel intimidated by a salesman
or contractor, call in friends or
family as backup support while
you negotiate.

143 ✳ Pay only after materials have been
delivered and work done. Never
pay the bill in full until the job is
finished to your liking.

144 ❋ Refuse to be pressured.

145 ❋ Get every important agreement or estimate in writing.

146 ❋ *"A verbal agreement isn't worth the paper it's written on."*
Samuel Goldwyn

147 ✳ Avoid pledging charitable contributions to telephone solicitors. Ask them to mail you information.

148 ✳ Recognize high-pressure sales tactics and walk away from them.

149 ✳ Be wary about giving out your credit card number over the phone.

150 ✳ Never show your eagerness to buy or sell.

151 ✳ Don't make major decisions without sleeping on them.

152 ✳ Eighty percent of all bad decisions are made in a hurry.

153 ✻ Rely on your instinct, but back it up with facts.

154 ✻ *"At twenty years of age, the will reigns; at thirty, the wit; and at forty, the judgment."*

Henry Grattan

155 ✳ "Older but wiser" is just wishful thinking, unless you make it happen.

156 ✳ *"It is costly wisdom that is bought by experience."*

Roger Ascham

157 ✳ Appreciate how much more you know today than you did years ago.

158 ✳ Share what you've learned over the years. There are those who will find your advice valuable.

159 ✳ A raisin is just a grape with experience.

160 ✳ Wrinkles are a natural process... just ask a prune.

161 ❄ Smile — it gives all those wrinkles a good excuse for being there.

162 ❄ Smile lines are not wrinkles.

163 ❄ Grin first... and then "bearing it" will come easy.

164 ❋ What, me worry?

165 ❋ There are very few worries that wouldn't be better off saved till tomorrow.

166 ❋ *"I've had a lot of problems in my day— most of which never happened."*
> Mark Twain

167 ✳ Control what you can in life; accept what you can't.

168 ✳ Take a deep breath. Let it out slowly. Then relax your body from the head and neck on down.

169 ✳ Plan some quiet time each day.

170 ※ If you have time to give to others, share generously. But keep your "alone" time sacred.

171 ※ Keep a weekly appointment book; it sets a value on your time.

172 ※ Time is a precious commodity; don't be afraid to say no.

173 ❋ Give yourself time to grow.

174 ❋ When it comes to **growing older**, you don't have much choice; when it comes to **growing**, the decision to grow or not to grow is entirely up to you.

175 ❋ You **can** teach an old dog new tricks.

176 ✳ Become computer literate — you're not too old.

177 ❋ Set challenges for yourself - as well as goals.

178 ❋ Learn to dance.

179 ❋ Take up photography.

180 ❋ Think twice before turning down the chance for a new experience.

181 ✳ Spend time outside every day, if at all possible.

182 ✳ *"There really is no such thing as bad weather, only different kinds of good weather."*

John Ruskin

183 ✳ Go fly a kite.

184 ✳ Walk, walk, walk... then walk a little more each day.

185 ✳ Borrow a dog to accompany you on walks if you don't have one.

186 ✳ Develop a late-blooming elevator phobia — use the stairs.

187 ❊ Hope to be healthy but do all you can to slant the odds in your favor.

188 ❊ Weight-bearing exercises like walking, jogging and bicycling can help slow down your rate of bone loss.

189 ❊ *Think* healthy.

190 ✳ Recognize healthy foods; avoid the unhealthy. Be sensible, but nobody expects you to be a saint.

191 ✳ *"One should eat to live, not live to eat."*
Moliere

192 ✳ Buy a good lowfat cookbook.

193 ❊ Learn how to calculate the percentage of calories from fat in your diet. Keep that percentage low — no more than 30%.

194 ❊ Some things our parents taught us just don't work today. Take time to re-evaluate old habits and ideas.

195 ✳ *"How many things we held yesterday as articles of faith which today we tell as fables."*

Michel de Montaigne

196 ✳ A healthy diet can delay or reverse many of the physical problems of aging: loss of muscle, and bone, as well as fat gain.

197 ❋ Studies show that fiber from grains, legumes, fruits and vegetables helps prevent a wide range of diseases. Most of us eat far too little fiber.

198 ❋ Take a healthy cooking class to update your skills and food awareness.

199 ✳ Weigh yourself once a week.

200 ✳ Even a modest weight loss can often lower blood pressure.

201 ✳ Mom was right — an apple a day keeps the doctor away. Five servings a day of fruits and vegetables are recommended.

202 ✳ Remember that your body's need for calories diminishes as you get older. If you'd rather not gain weight, you'll have to eat a little less as the years go by.

203 ✳ Exercise more! You'll burn more calories and maintain your weight.

204 ❋ Don't you owe it to yourself to do all you can to look and feel your best? It's never too late to start.

205 ❋ All too often old age is when you know your way around but don't feel like going.

206 ❋ Be kind to yourself!

207 ✳ *"Bald as the bare mountain tops are bald,
with a baldness full of grandeur."*
Matthew Arnold

208 ✳ The cheapest way to deal with a hair
loss problem is with a broom and
dustpan.

209 ❋ Love yourself.

210 ❋ Who says you have to be perfect?

211 ❋ Who says your spouse has to be perfect?

212 ❋ Count your blessings — consider the alternative.

213 ❋ *Older* is often *better*, just like old
friends, old wine, aged cheddar, old
times and the good old days.

214 ❋ Besides, everyone knows old age is
always years older than you are.

215 ❋ Have you done anything fun today?
You're never too old for fun.

216 ✳ Play a game you haven't played since childhood.

217 ✳ Share jokes.

218 ✳ Learn to whistle.

219 ✳ Take up a new sport — golf, walking, tennis, kayaking.

220 ✻ Test-drive a bright red convertible.
Go for it!

221 ✻ Feed the birds.

222 ✻ Wave at children.

223 ✻ Cuddle your cat. Incidentally, it's
said that pet owners live longer.

224 ✳ Share a sunrise.

225 ✳ Share your courage.

226 ✳ *"A hero is no braver than an ordinary man, but he is brave five minutes longer."*

R.W. Emerson

227 ✳ Courage is 99% experience.

228 ❋ *"Common sufferings are far stronger links than common joys."*

Lamartine

229 ❋ One hug speaks a thousand words.

230 ❋ *"In all misfortunes, the greatest consolation is a sympathizing friend."*

Cervantes

231 ✳ A true friend is not afraid to be needed.

232 ✳ People with close, caring friends are more likely to survive a heart attack or major illness than those without.

233 ✳ Recognize the difference between "alone" and "lonely".

234 ✳ Depression is common in older people, but it may be easily treated and cured. Learn its symptoms.

235 ✳ There are many possible causes of depression, some as simple to cure as a drug reaction, too little exercise or a nutritional deficiency. Tell your doctor if you suspect that you may be depressed

236 ✳ Some people are too busy helping others to have time to worry about problems of their own.

237 ✳ *"I want to live each minute*
With courage, zest and grace,
Thus keeping up the standard
Of the famous human race."
Rebecca McCann

238 ✻ *"Ask yourself whether you are happy and you cease to be so."*

John Stuart Mill

239 ✻ Follow the advice you probably gave your kids: Happy is as happy does.

240 ✻ Take a pottery class or dabble in oil paints.

241 ❋ Appreciate today's youth — you'll be older tomorrow.

242 ❋ *"Some folks are wise, and some are otherwise."*

Tobias Smollett

243 ❋ With age comes wisdom; call your mother.

244 ❋ *"Grief can take care of itself but to get the full value from joy, you must have somebody to divide it with."*

Mark Twain

245 ❋ Send lots of cards and notes to family and friends.

246 ❋ Look up a long-lost friend.

247 ✳ Remember your neighbors'
anniversaries, birthdays and special
occasions.

248 ✳ Make new friends.

249 ✳ *"No quality will get a man more friends
than a disposition to admire the
qualities of others."*

Boswell

250 ❋ Treat other people the way you
      expect to be treated.

251 ❋ Never argue when you're angry —
      words said in the heat of an
      argument almost always come back
      to haunt you.

252 ❋ You don't have to win every battle.

253 ✳ Don't argue about **who's** right —
determine **what's** right.

254 ✳ If you've never learned the fine art of
apologizing, it's time!

255 ✳ You're never too old to change your
opinion.

256 ✳ *"It wasn't until quite late in life that I discovered how to say, 'I don't know.'"*
Somerset Maugham

257 ✳ What do you want to be when you grow older? Why not give it a try right now?

258 ✳ Start an intriguing new business.

259 ✳ Don't think of retirement as your
license to sit around and do nothing
with your life. Set new goals for
yourself.

260 ✳ Add a new word to your vocabulary
each week.

261 ✳ Read a classic.

262 ✳ Learn about other religions; visit various churches, temples, synagogues and other places of worship.

263 ✳ Take a course in self-defense.

264 ❋ Retirement: a time when you never do all the things you intended to do when you had time.

265 ❋ Learn a new joke each week.

266 ❋ Study something you've never tried before: acting, singing, algebra or a new language.

267 ✳ Try something new and different each week?

268 ✳ Take a course in public speaking.

269 ✳ Don't be afraid of new experiences.

270 ✳ Aim a little high; if you aim too low, you'll never hit the bullseye.

271 ❋ Take a stand on political issues and
learn enough to defend your
position.

272 ✳ Keep current and you'll always have
    something interesting to talk about.

273 ✳ *"Sir, you have but two topics, yourself
    and me. I am sick of both."*
                            Dr. Samuel Johnson

274 ✳ Get down on the floor when you talk
    to a toddler.

275 ✳ Talk to neighborhood children.

276 ✳ In old age you're always someone's hero. Find that someone.

277 ✳ Never turn down a hug.

278 ✳ Accept help with a smile when it's offered.

279 ❋ Learn to say thank you.

280 ❋ Recycle love: send those hugs and
kisses back out there for another
round of usefulness.

281 ❋ *"An old man in love is like a flower in
winter."*

Portuguese proverb

282 ❋ Practice safe sex.

283 ❋ Spend the day in bed with someone you love.

284 ❋ If nothing surprises or delights you these days, then maybe you really are getting old.

285 ❋ Remember your love's favorite flower.

286 ❋ Compliment your spouse every day.

287 ❋ Turn off the TV and eat together.

288 ❋ Take turns giving each other massages.

289 ✻ Pamper yourself often — you deserve it. Just don't spoil yourself rotten in the process!

290 ✻ Soak your feet in a deliciously warm, scented bath.

291 ✻ Keep a tall stool to sit on while you work in the kitchen.

292 ❋ Your body's kept you going all these years. Treat it with respect in its old age.

293 ❋ C'mon now... up and at it! You've gotta exercise more than just caution.

294 ❋ "Running amok" doesn't necessarily qualify as exercise.

295 ❋ Always take the stairs even if you only do one flight.

296 ❋ Stand up a little straighter.

297 ❋ Treat yourself to a manicure.

298 ❋ Try a new haircut or style.

299 ✳ Dress to please yourself.

300 ✳ Wear colors that make you feel good.

301 ✳ Have a color analysis done. Our coloring changes as we age and colors that suited us earlier may not be flattering now.

302 ❋ Brush your teeth often.

303 ❋ Spend money on your mouth; keep your teeth well cared for.

304 ❋ Don't worry about what others think. At your age, you've earned the right to be Numero Uno, Top Dog, The Boss. Accept the position!

305 ✳ Do what you like, but like what you do.

306 ✳ Being old means never having to say you're forty.

307 ✳ Maintain a basic routine; without it, 'special' days won't feel special.

308 ✻ Keep an eye on your budget.

309 ✻ Be generous if you have it. Want to
be remembered as a world-class
penny-pincher?

310 ✻ *"In spite of the high cost of living, it's
still popular."*
Kathleen Norris

311 ❋ Are you "house rich and cash poor"?
Call your local HUD office or the
AARP and ask for information
about Reverse Annuity Mortgages.
Your house may be able to pay you
an income while you live in it!

312 ❋ Avoid adjustable-rate loans if your
income is fixed.

313 ✳ Are you 55 or older and selling your home? Ask your accountant if this would be the best time to use your $125,000 capital gain exclusion.

314 ✳ Does your state allow senior citizens to defer property tax payments until after you move from your home? Ask your local tax assessor.

315 ❋ Be savvy about money matters. Take a course in financial planning.

316 ❋ Don't hesitate to accept a senior citizens' discount.

317 ❋ Shop for groceries on a full stomach. You'll avoid temptation purchases, save money and buy more wisely.

318 ❋ Have lunch at an expensive restaurant. Lunches often cost less than dinners.

319 ❋ Beware of so-called "healthy" menu items that are actually high in fat.

320 ❋ Eat leafy green salads often; ask for dressing to be served on the side.

321 ✻ Plant a garden, even if you only
have space for a small windowbox.

322 ❋ Tend a garden for a busy family and share the bounty.

323 ❋ With gardening, you're a Triple Crown winner: you get fresh air, exercise and healthy food.

324 ❋ Learn a new style of eating— explore healthy options.

325 ❋ Have a complete physical check-up each year.

326 ❋ Ask your doctor's advice before making diet and exercise changes.

327 ❋ Don't call doctors, dentists or vets on Monday unless it's urgent; that's usually their busiest day.

328 ✳ Take a refresher course in CPR.

329 ✳ It's your body; don't hesitate to seek a second — or third — opinion.

330 ✳ In old age, good planning pays off. When you bend down to tie your shoes, for instance, plan something else to do while you're down there.

331 ✳ *"All would live long, but none would be old."*

Benjamin Franklin

332 ✳ Make a will.

333 ✳ *"Death is not the end; there remains the litigation."*

Ambrose Bierce

334 ✳ If you work too hard at saving for a rainy day, you won't have time to enjoy the sunshine.

335 ✳ Enjoy the money you've earned.

336 ✳ Don't wait until you can do a job perfectly, just do it now as well as reasonably possible.

337 ❋ Your word means something to others. Always keep your promises and it will mean a lot more.

338 ❋ Accept responsibility for your words and actions.

339 ❋ There's a world of difference between *I can't* and *I'll try*.

340 ❋ *"Everyone has talent at 25. The difficulty is to have it at 50."*

Edgar Degas

341 ❋ Keep your handshake firm — even if all else softens.

342 ❋ *Retirement* is not a synonym for *vacation*, nor should it be.

343 ❋ *"Those whom the gods love grow young."*
Oscar Wilde

344 ❋ Or is it this way:
*"Whom the gods love die young, no
matter how long they live."*
Elbert Hubbard

345 ✳ *"I am not young enough to know everything."*

J.M. Barrie

346 ✳ Young adults most admire older people who have managed to combine the wisdom of the ages with an astute knowledge of current events.

347 ❋ Talk about books you've enjoyed.

348 ❋ *"Choose a special book to read to a child. When I was very young, my grandfather read me* <u>Peter Rabbit</u> *at least a thousand times and I've remembered it — and him — so well after all these years."*

M.I. Wiser

349 ❋ Listen to the ideas and goals of your grandchildren.

350 ❋ Your children are raised, for better or worse. It's a 'done deal', so quit fretting about whether or not you did a good job.

351 ❋ Learn to congratulate yourself.

352 ✳ Stay involved with your community.

353 ✳ Support businesses in your neighborhood.

354 ✳ Know your neighbors.

355 ✳ When you move to a new home or apartment, have the locks changed.

356 ✳ Have a peephole put in your door.

357 ✳ Never feel obligated to open a door
when a stranger knocks.

358 ✳ Don't be timid about asking to see
identification.

359 ✳ Keep aware and up to date on issues that affect older people.

360 ✳ Join one of the many fine national associations for seniors. Membership often includes excellent literature, political clout, and group benefits. Ask a librarian for names and addresses.

361 ❋ *"An old man gives good advice to console himself for no longer being able to set a bad example."*
> Duc de la Rochefoucauld

362 ❋ It's never too late to set a good example.

363 ❋ Know when **not** to give advice.

364 ✳ Always be the last one to end a hug.

365 ✳ Be your own best friend.

366 ✳ *"To me, fair friend, you can never be old,*
for as you were when first your eye I
eyed, such seems your beauty still."

William Shakespeare

367 ✳ Re-watch an old movie with a friend
and re-live your past.

368 ✳ Don't live in the past. Enjoy today.

369 ✳ Never start the day by reading the obituaries.

370 ✳ Keep your mind in "forward" gear.

371 ✳ Old age is when your regrets are for those sins you **didn't** commit.

372 ❋ You've lived through a lot of history; write down your memories of historical events.

373 ❋ *"People will never look forward to posterity who never look backward to their ancestors."*

Edmund Burke

374 ❋ Plan to leave your heirs your most valuable assets: your thoughts, ideas, hopes, fears and dreams. Write or record them now.

375 ❋ How will you be remembered? That part of the script hasn't been written yet. How do you want to be remembered?

376 ✳ Keep a pad and pencil beside your
     bed to jot down thoughts that
     would otherwise keep you awake.

377 ✳ Or keep a tape recorder by your bed
     for elusive midnight memories.

378 ✳ Have a project ready to work on for
     an hour when you can't sleep.

379 ❋ Don't let little things get you down;
focus on the dollars, not the cents;
the hours, not the minutes; the
elephants, not the fleas.

380 ❋ *"There are two means of refuge from the
miseries of life: music and art."*
Albert Schweitzer

381 ✳ Learn to laugh when things go wrong. You'll get plenty of practice as you work your way through old age.

382 ✳ Today's problem is tomorrow's opportunity.

383 ✳ Laugh hard at least once a day.

384 ✳ Keep a cassette or two of really rollicking, uplifting music handy — Sousa marches, Chopin's waltzes, ragtime, revival hymns, showtunes or whatever makes you feel terrific.

385 ✳ Turn the radio up good and loud, then sing along.

386 ❋ Whistle while you work.

387 ❋ *"I find we are growing serious and then
we are in great danger of being dull."*
William Congreve

388 ❋ Think lively.

389 ❋ Find new and better ways to do things. There's always room for improvement.

390 ❋ Couples: re-evaluate your individual responsibilites or duties frequently. Re-assign, if it would make the load more even.

391 ✳ If you've stopped changing, you've stopped growing.

392 ✳ Give your retired spouse some time alone.

393 ✳ Take time away from your spouse to develop your own interests and friends.

394 ✳ *"Many men die at twenty-five and aren't buried until they are seventy-five."*
Ben Franklin

395 ✳ *"Few persons know how to be old."*
Duc de la Rochefoucauld

396 ✳ We do not stop laughing because we grow old; we grow old because we stop laughing.

INDEX

Half Wisdom *Half Wit*

The User's Guide Series from One More Press

A USER'S GUIDE TO A BETTER BOD
Wisdom for Facing the Trials of Creating a Healthier, Happier You   ISBN 0-941361-96-9 $6.50

A USER'S GUIDE TO LIVING WITH PETS
Wisdom for Facing the Trials of Living with Dogs and Cats   ISBN 0-941361-95-0 $6.50

A USER'S GUIDE TO LOVE
Wisdom for Facing the Trials of Intimate Relationships   ISBN 0-941361-97-1 $6.50

A USER'S GUIDE TO MONEY
Wisdom for Facing the Trials of Making, Keeping and Spending It   ISBN 0-941361-94-2 $6.50

A USER'S GUIDE TO OLD AGE
Wisdom for Facing the Trials of Growing Older   ISBN 0-941361-98-5 $6.50

A USER'S GUIDE TO PARENTHOOD
Wisdom for Facing the Trials of Raising Kids   ISBN 0-941361-99-3 $6.50

These lighthearted books by Jo Elder and M.I. Wiser are available at bookstores and gift shops everywhere. If you are unable to find them locally, they may be ordered by mail from the publisher, One More Press, P.O. Box 1885, Lake Oswego, OR 97035. Please enclose a check or money order for the cost of the books plus $2.50 per order for shipping and handling.

ABOUT THE AUTHORS

Jo Elder and M.I.Wiser have spent the better part of two lifetimes handing out advice, in a style that's wise and witty.

Just like the readers of their **User's Guides** and popular advice column, *Half Wisdom / Half Wit*, Jo and M.I. have personally dealt with many of life's challenges. Between them, they've lived through two successful marriages and one bitter divorce. They've suffered the loss of close family members, fought and won the daily battle against weight gain and dealt with the problems involved in raising childen (and pets) in today's high-pressure world. Jo and M.I., who live in Oregon, have attended college, had successful careers and created profitable businesses. They are the authors of more than two dozen books.

Jo and M.I. like to think of their **User's Guides** as instruction manuals for surviving life's most common, but troublesome, situations.